THE SAINT OF FUCKED-UP KARMA

THE SAINT OF FUCKED-UP KARMA:

A MUSICAL

Paul R. Abramson

ASYLUM 4 RENEGADES PRESS
Joshua Tree, California

ASYLUM 4 RENEGADES PRESS
Joshua Tree, California
asylum4renegadespress.com

A4R seeks daring projects of interest to academic and educated readers. A4R admires risk-taking authors who write with intelligence and grace while remaining self-effacing and wryly humorous.

Paul R. Abramson
abramsonuclapsych.com

Cover art and book design
Tania Love Abramson

Copy Editor
Vici Casana

First Edition

Copyright 2017 Paul R. Abramson
ISBN: 978-0692893289

Praise for

The Saint of Fucked-Up Karma

Abramson is a national treasure.

—Drex Heikes, *LA Weekly*

In this Greek tragedy reinvented as an American rock musical, the shock of an original sin triggers waves of evil that batter human lives. Tossed by these turbulent waters, love, trust, and individual responsibility are nearly drowned but somehow—almost miraculously—manage to tread water still.

—Keith Holyoak, author of *The Gospel According to Judas*

Abramson's Saint *is a striking work based closely on horrific real events he encountered as an expert witness. The narrative blends fully with the music, which in turn captures the energy and anguish of the story.*

—Gregory A. Miller, Distinguished Professor and Chair, Department of Psychology, UCLA

Praise for Previous Books by
PAUL R. ABRAMSON

Abramson, P.R. (2017). *Screwing Around with Sex:*
Essays, Indictments, Anecdotes and Asides. **Joshua Tree, CA:**
Asylum 4 Renegades Press.

I have, at times, insisted that the lives of sex researchers are pretty boring. Paul Abramson's collection of analytical essays, Screwing Around With Sex, *reveals that this is not always the case. Drawing on personal experiences and preoccupations necessitated by decades of scholarly investigation of sexuality, Abramson highlights the uneasy and sometimes painful interface of sexuality with our current moral landscape. In doing so, he elucidates the contradictions and complexities of contemporary sexuality in ways that frustrate, challenge, and inspire us to question our preconceived notions of what sexuality is—or should be.*
—Dr. Terri Conley, Professor of Psychology and Women's Studies, University of Michigan

The mix of effective anecdotes with the process of grappling with moral/scientific issues is very compelling. Chapter 3 ("On the Precipice of Porn") reminded me of David Foster Wallace's book Consider the

Lobster, *in particular, Wallace's first chapter on the adult video industry.*

—Dr. Keith Holyoak, Distinguished Professor of Psychology, UCLA, and Editor of *Psychological Review*

Professor Abramson has made issues that are difficult, ancient, and current accessible without oversimplifying; urgent policy challenges tractable; and profound experiences understandable. Over and over as you read, you think, "Yes, we need to act."

—Dr. Gregory A. Miller, Distinguished Professor and Chair, Department of Psychology, UCLA

An idiosyncratic page-turner of a personal and professional journey that brought Paul Abramson to the heart of some of the most interesting issues of sexuality and sexual abuse in the late twentieth century and—through his role as a psychology professor serving as an expert witness—to the back stage of some of the nation's most important obscenity cases. Enjoyable and illuminating.

—Catherine Ross, Professor of Law, George Washington University Law School

Abramson, P. R. (2010). *Sex Appeal: Six Ethical Principles for the 21st Century*. New York, NY: Oxford University Press.

What a great idea. . . . I completely agree with Abramson. . . . I do wish that more literature on the subject resembled [his] book.
   —The New Yorker

*Very interesting . . . so interesting I may have to do multiple posts about it. So interesting that I was pissed when I just spilled coffee on it, because this is one book I plan to keep. . . . [In fact,] we could start a sexual revolution right here, through this blog, with help from **this** book.*
   —Marie Claire

Sex Appeal *is the beginning of a conversation that has been a long time coming. How can people make safe, ethical choices about sex without sacrificing the fun of it? How can these choices make our lives, and the world, a better place? Paul Abramson explores these questions and more with six key concepts that will help readers to better understand how to prevent sexual harm while safely enjoying all of the benefits sex has to offer.* **Sex Appeal** *is provocative and refreshing in its embrace of a kind of sexual freedom that is at once both joyful and thoughtful.*
   —Dr. Ruth Westheimer (Dr. Ruth)

[**Sex Appeal**] *is really smart, interesting, and honest.*

—Nathan Schiller, Editor, *Construction Literary* Magazine

While it's unlikely to happen, [**Sex Appeal**] *should probably be part of the curriculum of every high school sex ed class. . . . [T]o a young person, the insights (or at least the lessons attached to them) could be huge.*

—*Feminist Review*

[Dr.] Abramson, an American professor of psychology and one of the most famous scholars of human sexuality, reminds us that the body is marching to the rhythm of the brain.

—*Le Regole Dell'Attrazione Magazine* (Italy)

Abramson, P. R. (2007). *Romance in the Ivory Tower: The Rights and Liberty of Conscience.* Cambridge, MA: MIT Press.

Make no mistake—Paul Abramson's book is a serious and thought-provoking examination of the extent to which institutions should proscribe individual actions. Although I do not endorse all of the conclusions, I strongly recommend this book.

—Lord Robert May, Oxford University

Romance in the Ivory Tower *presents a compelling argument about the erosion of the rights of privacy and conscience. The debate in this book transcends the issue of personal relationships within academia and engages fundamental questions of liberty and personal choice.*

—**Nadine Strossen, President, American Civil Liberties Union**

Abramson, P. R., Pinkerton, S. D., & Huppin, M. (2003).
***Sexual Rights in America: The Ninth Amendment and the Pursuit of Happiness.* New York: NYU Press.**

This frank and lucid book peels the fig leaf off various forms of legal regulation of sexuality and argues with passion and rich historical detail that individuals should have strong autonomy over their sexual expression as long as their sexual relationships are grounded in consent. The authors' comprehensive approach makes a considerable contribution to the literature.

—**Kathleen Sullivan, Dean, Stanford Law School**

Abramson, P. R., & Pinkerton, S. D. (2000). *A House Divided: Suspicions of Mother–Daughter incest.* **New York, NY: Norton.**

A riveting true story . . . meticulous and engaging.
> —**Publisher's Weekly**

Abramson, P. R., & Pinkerton, S. D. (1995). *With Pleasure: Thoughts on the Nature of Human Sexuality.* **New York, NY: Oxford University Press.**

Stimulating, and informative, and written with ample wit.
> —*Scientific American*

A fresh and theoretically enticing approach to the study of human sexuality . . . Sure to spark intense debate.
> —*Kirkus Reviews*

Provocative.
> —*Seattle Times*

Abramson, P. R., & Pinkerton, S. D. (1995). (Eds.) *Sexual Nature/ Sexual Culture*. **Chicago, IL: University of Chicago Press.**

This volume contains much to stimulate, inform, and amuse, in varying proportions. What more can one ask?
> **—Journal of the History of Sexuality**

If we ever expect to solve the sexuality-based problems that modern societies face, we must encourage investigations of human sexual behavior. Moreover, those investigations should employ a broad range of disciplines—looking at sex from all angles, which is precisely what **Sexual Nature/ Sexual Culture** *does.*
> **—American Scientist**

Highly informative. . . .[T]here is none other quite like it.
> **—Choice**

It is useful to find this interesting question scientifically settled once and for all.
> **—Times Literary Supplement**

Illuminating.
> **—Gay Times**

Intriguing.

—**Feminist Collections**

This book goes a long way towards bridging the gap between nature and nurture.

—**New Scientist**

Abramson, P. R. (1984). *Sarah: A Sexual Biography.*
Albany, NY: State University of New York Press.

How can so much intimate, destructive violence be part of our here and now, almost before our eyes? No novelist would dare, because fiction can neither resolve, nor even make reasonable, this material.

—**The Los Angeles Times**

A fascinating account . . . . A brief but memorable view of emotional survival.

—**Booklist**

(the author)

photo by Sienna Bland-Abramson

Lyrics:
Paul R. Abramson
shestabbedmoses.com

Music:
Paul Abramson, Robin Finck, & Crying 4 Kafka
crying4kafka.com

Musical Arrangement and Performance:
Crying 4 Kafka
vendingmachinesound.com

Illustrations:
Paul R. Abramson

Story & Dramaturgical Consultants:

Annaka Abramson, Sienna Bland-Abramson,
Tania Love Abramson, Marc Bobro, Paul du Gre,
Melanie Eckford-Prossor, Robin Finck, Joanna Folino,
Drex Heikes, Keith Holyoak, Mike Kresky, Bill Lewis,
Dan Linz, Gregory A. Miller, Ian Putnam, Bianca Sapetto,
Brandon Thibeault, Polly Walker, and Linda Williamson

Clubs and Theaters:

The Saint of Fucked-Up Karma was staged on four
occasions at Club Fais Do Do in Los Angeles, California
in 2013. *The Saint of Fucked-Up Karma* was also staged on
four occasions in 2013 in Santa Barbara, California, twice
at Muddy Waters Café, and once at Center Stage Theater
and West Coast Books. Bill Lewis, Simon Taylor, and
Steven Yablok were steadfast exemplars of benevolence.

This musical is based on a true story — a civil lawsuit involving a police officer caught in the act of raping a 13-year-old boy.

photo by Sienna Bland-Abramson

Crying 4 Kafka (2013)

Paul Abramson (vocals and lyrics), Mattia Bacca (rhythm guitar), Marc Bobro (bass), Ian Putnam (lead guitar), and Brandon Thibeault (drums)

photo by Tania Love Abramson

Crying 4 Kafka (2016)

Paul Abramson (vocals and lyrics), Marc Bobro (bass),
Bryan Kovarick (drums), and Ian Putnam (guitar)

DEDICATION

Richard C. Bennett
and
the late Robert Bruce Galler

The Saint of Fucked-Up Karma,
So dark from within,
Preaching the truth
At the crossroads of our sins.

(Lyrics from the song titled "The Saint of Fucked-Up Karma," from the musical of the same name)

ONE ACT

This is a one-act musical with 14 scenes. Songs do not burst forth from actors but are instead performed by Crying 4 Kafka as punctuation marks.

Curtains open prior to Scene 1 and close following the reprise (the song **Whole Lotta Love** rewritten for this musical as **Hell of a Love**). Running time is approximately 70 minutes.

CHARACTERS

DR. FRANK MATTHEWS An expert witness in criminal and civil litigation. He sings baritone in a free-spirited gospel choir.

KEELY A set designer for a Netflix Original series. She is Frank Matthews's recalcitrant girlfriend.

THE COMMENTATOR A Shakespearean actor in Elizabethan costume.

MUSIC

There are eight songs and one reprise. They can be heard in various iterations on the Crying 4 Kafka bootleg CD *The Frank Recordings* and the DVD of *The Saint of Fucked-Up Karma Soundtrack* and as Crying 4 Kafka songs on iTunes. A studio soundtrack CD is also being recorded at Vending Machine Sound.

STAGING

The stage is designed for monologues and intimate dialogue. Lighting and positioning augment each scene. Props are discretionary, minimal usage is advised.

When actors are performing, Crying 4 Kafka is behind a curtain. The curtain is drawn only when actors leave the stage. Crying 4 Kafka then performs songs in their absence.

THE COMMENTATOR introduces the musical and speaks directly to the audience throughout. **THE COMMENTATOR** is the thread that binds the musical together.

THE SAINT OF FUCKED-UP KARMA

THE COMMENTATOR:

Have you ever seen the northern lights?

I was standing with my daughter on a hilltop in Reykjavik. It was around midnight. A young couple was pointing upward. Fleeting green tendrils, tinged with muted radiance, maneuvered across the sky.

So much of life is chance. Some things you see; some you don't. Some by choice, some not. An insurmountable fissure between what we expect and what we get, premonition forever overshadowing comprehension, and chips never falling as they may.

Scene 1

DR. FRANK MATTHEWS (Begins his monologue about Porter Jones):

People tell me that I'm a saint for getting involved in these cases. I've never seen it that way. I'm just better at staying detached.

It's not necessarily a blessing, and it's not always a curse.

(Pauses) His name was Porter Jones. He was 13 years old. His mother, Dolly, was a prostitute; and his father, Jake, was a bank robber who had OD'd on heroin soon after he got out of jail.

Dolly was done. Done with dope. Done with bank robbers. Done with Johns. She had moved to a tiny town near Sedona, Arizona, to get away from it all. She thought she had it made when a friendly cop, Tim Tully, took an interest in her son.

(**DR. MATTHEWS** acts this part out)

How old are you?

13.

That's close enough. Come on! Want to join the Police Explorers? Ya get a uniform, a badge. Teach you to shoot a gun. You ever shot a gun? Fun as hell!

No! But yeah! said Porter.

Three months go by. Porter is in the Explorers, and Tim Tully lavishes Dolly with gifts, a laptop, all kinds of stuff.

Then one night Tully asks Dolly:

(**DR. MATTHEWS** acts this part out)

Hey, I'm having a barbecue. Next Friday night. We got tri-tip. We're gonna ride ATVs. My old girlfriend'll be there. Can Porter come? It'll be great! He can spend the night.

Dolly thinks, Sure, that's fine; he's a cop.

Tim Tully has the barbecue, they eat tri-tip, they ride the ATVs, but at ten thirty, Tully's old girlfriend leaves.

Sixteen miles later her car breaks down. Tully's house is closer than Flagstaff, so she has it towed back to his home.

Something's not quite right. Sheets are covering the windows. She uses her key to open the front door and walks inside.

Right there on the couch Tim Tully is raping Porter Jones.

Tully jumps up. Grabs his gun. Puts it to her head.

She WAILS. Just WAILS.

He puts the gun to his own head. She WAILS even louder.

Tully throws down the gun, calls his department chief, and confesses.

CRYING 4 KAFKA performs the song "CONTEMPLATING WHORES AGAIN"

THE COMMENTATOR:

Frank and Keely pretend, as you'll soon discover, that everything is stationary, set in stone, never letting change galvanize them, preferring instead a repetitive discourse that comforts in a mindless kind of way.

(Pauses) Why have I been assigned to this role? I'm not righteous. I struggle no less than the next person.

Scene 2

KEELY: Do you ever get burned out?

DR. MATTHEWS: What do ya mean?

KEELY: Your crazy childhood. The world of trauma?

DR. MATTHEWS: I'd beware of pity.

KEELY: Pity? It's not pity. It's concern. Your life is enshrined in grief. (Pauses) I know you're fighting for something. Who could miss that? But it all gets mixed up in a twisted kind of way.

(Dr. Frank Matthews)

DR. MATTHEWS: I give to these people.

KEELY: Your cases. But not to me. Or us.

DR. MATTHEWS: I see it differently. You thrive on hope. I don't. I don't believe in soul mates. Marriages made in heaven. I can't imagine how any of those things could yield happiness. I want none of it.

KEELY: What's wrong with soul mates?

DR. MATTHEWS: Nothing. Nothing. I just don't believe in them. I look around. Everyone is falling in or out of love. I'm done with it.

KEELY: That's depressing.

DR. MATTHEWS: The things I do, or try to do, are done because I think they're right. It's gotta feel right. Marriage seems like is a crapshoot. I don't like to gamble.

KEELY: Is it right between us?

DR. MATTHEWS: Definitely! Definitely!

KEELY: Then why'd you disappear? For three weeks? No calls. Nothing!

DR. MATTHEWS: I had no choice. I keep telling you that. I had no choice. This case . . .

KEELY: You're always on cases.

DR. MATTHEWS: Not like this one. Cop raping a kid. Can you imagine? Mother is a prostitute. He needed help.

KEELY: We need help.

DR. MATTHEWS: That cop knew exactly what he was doing. This family had billboards on their backs: *WOUNDED BIRDS.*

KEELY: I don't doubt that. None of it. But it's beside the point. We're a sinking ship. We deserve better.

DR. MATTHEWS: We're not sinking. Just because I don't feel the way you do doesn't mean that I care any less. (Pauses) You're an artist. You always see things differently. (Pauses) I never know what to do — keep talking or go for a walk. (Pauses) It's not for the lack of trying. I just never know what to do. I can't figure it out.

THE COMMENTATOR:

Most people talk about feelings the way insurance brokers talk about the weather — dull and vaguely familiar. (Pauses) Like music in a dentist's office, carefully eviscerated, surviving only as totems to mediocrity.

Scene 3

DR. MATTHEWS (Begins a monologue about his childhood)**:**

I was in a terrible accident. I was eight years old. (Lifts his shirt to show the scar) Fifty stitches. The scar runs from below my belly button to my rib cage, and then it turns right, toward my back. It looks like a jagged lowercase *r*.

Now imagine it on an 8-year-old. And angry red.

I was standing on a five-foot ledge. I slipped and fell to the concrete below and was knocked unconscious. Another kid fell, too. His knees landed in my stomach. I was dead, or so he thought. He ran away.

When I woke up, I crawled home on both arms, dragging my body behind me, blood dripping from my mouth.

It freaked the hell out of my mother. An ambulance was called, and it took me to Saint Agatha's Hospital. The Emergency Room doctor looked like Sherlock Holmes — not the new actor, but the old one, Basil Rathbone. He was holding an enormous needle.

Frank, he whispered, *you won't feel a thing.*

I didn't.

But I did remember what my father said to me in the ambulance.

You know what the FUCK this is going to cost me?!

Run, Frank, run is all I could think.

**CRYING 4 KAFKA performs the song
"RUN, FRANK, RUN"**

(The Surgeon)

THE COMMENTATOR:

We build monuments, inadvertently, to suffering and courage — a collection of human voices offering testimony to lives lived, a cacophony of listless monologues, or perhaps searing personal testimonies, each unfolding from within.

Retelling personal histories is cathartic, even without worrying about validity or accountability. Collective memories can be molded, and memory itself is constructive.

Has Frank embellished the truth? Has it been streamlined to avoid complication and nuance? Or is it simply a myth converted into a story of heroic sacrifice and achievement?

Centuries ago St. Elmo's fire was a token from God signifying that a raging storm was about to pass. I've often wondered, for Frank and Keely's sake, if there might be a psychological equivalent heralding that the worst is behind them now.

Scene 4

DR. MATTHEWS: I know it sounds clichéd, but I'm in it to win.

KEELY: Is that how you define this? Win? At what cost?

DR. MATTHEWS: There's no cost. I'm not paying anything. If I don't believe in a case, I walk. I'm done.

KEELY: You're never done. You're the guardian angel of the odd, forever grabbing hold of unraveling threads of trauma.

DR. MATTHEWS: I'm not grabbing hold of anything. I get a call, and I take the case or not. It's a gut thing. Am I supposed to ignore that?

KEELY (Changes the subject): Are you having an affair?

DR. MATTHEWS: An affair? No. Not at all. One relationship is plenty.

KEELY: Like one dinner is plenty? That's comforting.

DR. MATTHEWS: What are you asking?

KEELY: I need something more.

DR. MATTHEWS: I don't know what to say. I feel like I'm being accused, obliquely at least, for not doing enough. Have I've missed the point? What do you want?

KEELY: I need something other than a prison with perks.

DR. MATTHEWS: Prison? I work hard. These are my people. I know it sounds ridiculous, but when I was a kid, I knew them by name. Drug addicts, the homeless, prostitutes.

KEELY: You ever get tired of this?

DR. MATTHEWS: Yeah, yeah. I get tired of it. Fed up.

KEELY: You've been at it for 18 years.

DR. MATTHEWS: I don't want to desert them. If it's down to me, so be it. Courtrooms are like tea parties compared to my home. (Pauses) I came from a messed-up family. I don't want to apologize for that.

KEELY: Nobody's asking you to apologize.

DR. MATTHEWS: Feels that way.

KEELY: Because I'm unhappy? With something you did? Or didn't do?

DR. MATTHEWS: You act like I can't measure up.

KEELY: It has nothing to do with measuring up. There's a wall around your heart.

DR. MATTHEWS: There's no wall.

KEELY: Concrete.

DR. MATTHEWS: I'm letting *you* in.

KEELY: Really? You can't even see the signs.

DR. MATTHEWS: What are you talking about?

KEELY: You never apologized!

DR. MATTHEWS: That kid needed me. I wasn't going to turn my back. That cop. In prison. He's been stabbed repeatedly with a fork, one time close to his heart. I don't even want to talk about the pictures I saw.

KEELY: You can't even talk about the feelings you have. Uncharted territory populated with vague regrets.

DR. MATTHEWS: (Sighs, shaking his head.) It's not easy juggling reprimands.

THE COMMENTATOR:

It's curious how we craft relationships of our own devising, acting as if our partners are mirrored images of ourselves.

I like complexity, as long as it serves authenticity and the quest for truth, however envisioned.

Scene 5

DR. MATTHEWS (Continues his monologue about Porter Jones):

After Tim Tully was sent to prison, a friendly DA told Dolly:

(**DR. MATTHEWS** acts this part out)

You ought to sue Tully — and the police department, too. Take the money and get help for Porter. He's gonna need it.

Dolly liked the sound of that, particularly the money part. Somehow she got a great Phoenix attorney, Hector Ramos. It was Mr. Ramos who retained me as the expert witness. My job was to figure out how this whole thing had unfolded, and what it had done to Porter.

Tully had been caught in the act, and then he confessed. The big question was whether the police department had known about his history of sexually abusing young boys — or more importantly — should have known about it.

We didn't know shit, they claimed. *Tully was a rogue cop doing crap on his own time, at his own place. You can't blame us.*

BULLSHIT, Porter said. *He was groping me in the cop car. In the bathroom at the station. On security patrols. All the time.*

(Pauses) Then Tim Tully wrote a letter from prison to his Police Chief:

I don't know what's wrong with me. I wish I knew. I'd get help. I was in so many foster homes. Stuff happened. It's no excuse. But I gotta tell you this. All that stuff with Porter happened on my own time, at my own place.

Bullshit! Porter said again.

The police department refused to settle the civil lawsuit. That forced Mr. Ramos and me to prove that the department should've known that Tim Tully was a sexually abusing cop.

It took us four years, but we discovered that Tully had previously been named as a molester in a murder trial in Phoenix. A MURDER trial! A 16-year-old homeless kid who was accused of murder had started crying on the stand: *I'm messed up — really messed up — because* (Pointing at Tim Tully) *that cop was having sex with me.*

Tully laughed. *Yeah, right,* he said. Other police officers laughed, too.

Three months later, Tim Tully was transferred, no questions asked, to that tiny town near Sedona, Arizona. He was *relocated,* just like they did with the sexually abusing Catholic priests.

Then we also discovered that Tully had been married before. His ex-wife had divorced him because he was bringing runaway boys to their home at night.

But the police department *still* refused to settle. Worse yet, Porter was getting arrested for breaking into houses, breaking into cars, stealing guns, alcohol. We'd plead with each and every judge to give Porter a break. He had been sexually abused by a police officer, we'd testify, assuring the judge that we'd soon get funds to underwrite a four-year full ride scholarship to a therapeutic high school.

Then Jonathan, a young man in Phoenix working in a Harley Davidson shop, materialized. Jonathan had been a Police Explorer, too. When he was 14, Tim Tully

(Tim Tully and foster mother in court)

molested him in the squad car, in the bathroom at the station, and on security patrol.

His story matched Porter's, but the cities were different. Jonathan knew nothing about Porter's case.

The police department then threw in the towel. Porter Jones received a million-dollar settlement.

Here's the sad part. Porter blew through the money in four years. There was no therapeutic high school. Nothing. One year after the money was gone, *Porter* was arrested and sentenced to a federal prison for armed robbery.

THE COMMENTATOR:

There are no calm voices and dim lights herein. Flames never gambol. These voices are shrill, and the light is startling, relentlessly so.

Scene 6

KEELY (Monologue): This guy is upset if I'm late for dinner.

(Keely)

I've got a girlfriend, Suzanne. Her father disappeared in the Bosnian War. Just disappeared and was never found.

Can you imagine what that feels like? Your father disappeared! Presumed dead. And never returns.

I'm working on a sculpture, stuff I found in the desert. It's a head that's been shattered like glass, but the pieces never quite fit. Reminds me of Frank.

I had no idea what to expect. I was scared. Waiting for a reckless savior with endless pride and no sense of time.

I had NO idea what to expect.

THE COMMENTATOR:

Nothing is fixed to a point. Public masks are exposed. Spooked perhaps, but necessarily so.

Though they believe themselves to be entitled by frustration and anger, reducing their actions to a necessary reflex and never troubled by ambiguity or doubt, Frank and Keely are nonetheless bowing down to the mighty gods of denial and certainty.

Scene 7

DR. MATTHEWS (Continues his monologue about his childhood):

My father had a twisted view of religion. It was a hammer. The God of Vengeance. He would scream about what is — and what isn't. Fuck this and fuck that. A haiku of hate, throwin' firecrackers at ghosts.

He despised every girlfriend I ever had. *Get rid of her. She's a slut.* Friends couldn't believe that he talked that way.

My father even once claimed that John the Baptist, of all people, said that vans were whorehouses on wheels. (Confiding to the audience) It should come as no surprise to learn that I, too, had a van.

But he never drank. He wasn't racist. He supported gays if they served in the military.

He just hated me.

**CRYING 4 KAFKA performs the song
"HOLY ROLLER"**

(Frank's van)

THE COMMENTATOR:

(Sings a capella)

There's blood in the rain, and it's starting again.

Crosses are pointing, and everyone's sinned.

They're burning a place where nobody escapes.

It's time for the one who determines his own fate.

Orpheus brought his wife back to life with music.
Mournful music. The riddle of unrequited love.

Scene 8

KEELY (Monologue):

He said he had a life filled with shadows. His father always telling him that he's *Outta his fuckin' mind,* or a *fuck-up,* then chasing him with golf clubs.

It's hard for me to hear that stuff. I had a good dad. We lived on a dairy farm. A crisis in our house was calling the vet at 3 in the morning.

He'd tell me it sounds like *Mary Poppins.*

Do I want to be part of his world? Can I sweep away that kind of agony?

THE COMMENTATOR:

Perhaps it's a relentless effort to understand, albeit in a Socratic kind of way, forever asking and then answering questions.

Is it possible for Keely to soar above intimacy and reason by envisioning the right question?

We are changed only by what we change.

Scene 9

DR. MATTHEWS (Continues his monologue about his childhood):

It's not like my mother was any help either. She was the back-up singer. The Greek chorus. *Don't argue with your father. Pray. Do better in school. Find the right girl. Get ready for college.*

College? My father flunked out of NYU. He was a business major. He didn't pass a single course, something that was kinda prophetic given his business acumen, a dilapidated liquor store.

CRYING 4 KAFKA performs the song "COMMUTERS LIQUOR STORE."

(Frank's father)

THE COMMENTATOR:

I had a melanoma. It was tiny. I never noticed it. My dermatologist caught it.

She didn't like the look of a mole on my left cheek. She cut it off and had it biopsied. It was cancer, she said, but she told me not to worry. We caught it early.

I didn't think much about it. I was reassured by her comments. When I went to the surgeon two weeks later to remove the surrounding tissue, I thought it would be a three-minute procedure. It had only taken seconds to remove the mole.

Then the surgeon drew a large triangle on my cheek. *That looks huge,* I said.

This is the protocol, she replied. *You cut out the tissue.*

She cut a vein, too; blood squirted all over my collar. Now I have a three-inch-long scar on my face. It's curious how things work out.

I remember driving down a deserted dirt road in Sardinia, near the town of Palmadula. A large goat ran in front of the car. It scared the hell out of us. Then we laughed, hearing the bell clanging up the mountain.

That was curious, too, in a different kind of way.

Scene 10

DR. MATTHEWS (Continuing his monologue):

Sometimes my mother was really sweet. And funny. We'd laugh so hard she'd cry, begging me to stop.

She never hugged me, though. When I left for college, she shook my hand.

(Frank's mother)

If perchance I complained about my father, she wouldn't talk. Eventually she'd deny everything. Or make excuses for him. *He works hard.*

I never knew what to expect from her.

CRYING 4 KAFKA performs the song "WIN BIG & LOSE IT ALL."

THE COMMENTATOR:

Some people believe that religion is a talismanic form of imprisonment that transforms disciples through ritualistic conventions.

Not that I know anything about religion. Hard on the knees, not to mention the psyche.

I celebrate the quirky (the Commentator encourages the audience to clap along to these comments), the unconventional (more clapping), those off-kilter perspectives (clapping) that shed light upon the pictorial problems (clapping) that demand our recognition (clapping).

We need those kinds of people (clapping), like you and me (louder clapping), people willing to stay faithful to the truth (clapping), even when it's dirty and inconvenient (more clapping).

Scene 11

KEELY (Monologue directed to the audience):

He's in a cage. He says he can get out. I don't know. He's restless. Holding on upside down.

Should I believe him? He never apologized. He didn't even say he missed me 'til I prompted him. Then, like a wounded love cry: "I DID miss you. I REALLY felt it!"

But he didn't say it 'til I asked him.

I know it's horrible what happened to that kid. But at some point you move on. Right? Frank keeps telling me there's a patina on madness. Is that an answer? To what?

THE COMMENTATOR:

There's no single constricting pattern of charred love and graces. No redemptive visions. Only curdling spirals have entangled them all.

Scene 12

DR. MATTHEWS (Completes his monologue about his childhood):

I know I seem normal, maybe to some of you. But as a kid, I was plotting to kill my father.

I'd imagine him backing me into a corner. Pinning me against the wall. In a panic, I reach for a knife on the counter. Stab him in the chest. I could feel it go right through him, striking bone.

You killed me, he says; then he dies.

Would I really do that? (Pauses) No, never. If I killed him, I'd have to live forever in the kingdom of the half-dead. That's a feeling that *never* goes away. (Pauses again) Even as a teenager, I knew that the past isn't always prologue.

**CRYING 4 KAFKA performs the song
"PUNCHING AT YOUR HEART"**

THE COMMENTATOR:

Do we really have choices? We spend so much time parsing observable causes that nothing ever seems left to chance, or better yet, discretion. Are life choices reducible to an ironclad psychic determinism? If so, why is that any different from a teleological explanation? Trading gods, it seems to me.

Science will prevail; it always does. But in the interim we are left with filling in the blanks to foreshadow the artifice of writing human lives. Underlying explanations are exchanged so that one or the other can triumph as the ultimate designer of it all.

(Pauses) I like to think that we make our own beds.

Scene 13

KEELY: Is that why you disappeared? Because of that cop?

DR. MATTHEWS: Not exactly.

KEELY: Well?

DR. MATTHEWS: Toward the end, I'm visiting Dolly. She lived in that trailer park near Sedona. Tall woman . . . covered with tattoos . . . no front teeth.

KEELY: Cute.

DR. MATTHEWS: Something like that. Anyway, she tells me this story — pointing to a bullet hole in her plate-glass window.

See that bullet hole. See it? Cops done this. They're trying to kill me. I know it. Nobody cares about an old whore.

KEELY: Geez.

DR. MATTHEWS: So I called the FBI. I was there for two days.

KEELY: Then what happened?

DR. MATTHEWS: I've told you I can't talk about that part.

KEELY: What? Witness Protection Program?

DR. MATTHEWS: I can't talk about it.

KEELY: I thought that was for snitching on the mob?

DR. MATTHEWS: I can't talk.

KEELY: Rogue cops, too, I guess. That makes sense. They were protecting people in LA from that cop who was hiding in Big Bear. Remember that?

DR. MATTHEWS: Yeah I remember.

KEELY: It's not because these pieces don't fit together. It's that I don't care anymore. I can't do this dance. I'm done. I'm sorry. I'm done.

DR. MATTHEWS: Done? What do you mean done? How is that fair?

KEELY: If you had called me to apologize. We do stupid things. Whatever. But you didn't even say you were sorry. Did you think I wouldn't be hurt? I can't live this way. Really. It's over.

DR. MATTHEWS: I don't want that. I *feel* for you.

KEELY: Feel for me? You mean LOVE me? You never change. Look at you. (Touching his necklace) Voodoo charm?

DR. MATTHEWS: (Looks at his necklace) I got it in New Orleans. (Tries to make a joke) I guess it didn't work. (Pauses) I'm going for a walk. (Pauses) A long walk.

KEELY: That's all you have to say?

DR. MATTHEWS: (with no emotion) I don't know what to say. I can't think.

CRYING 4 KAFKA performs the song

"HEY, I'M NOT SORRY."

(Dolly old and young)

THE COMMENTATOR:

(Sings a capella)

The Saint of Fucked-Up Karma paralyzed the street again;

Round and round and round he shouted, Eternity at 10.

We know that Faust was normal, but what about this sage?

Free to roam the boulevard but trapped inside a cage.

Trapped we are, no doubt, by smartphones, social media, and the like. Assailed and contaminated by the drivel of pundits and politicians, so-called celebrities even more so.

What are we celebrating? Random clichés and vacuous monologues, with canned laughter however conceived. These are all ultimately filler, each bowing to the whims of commerce. Selling and consuming are the undisputed Kings and Queens of America, despite appearances otherwise.

Public virtue is the armor of private vice. Every good deed begets another—consumer that is. That's the magic of advertising. Businesses that routinely package their products as somehow integral to an environmental cause, or a higher goal, only to then milk it shamelessly are no less a part of the problem. If you look closely at the labels on their products, they're all mass-produced in China or some other part of the world where human rights are synonymous with human wrongs.

Even the news is nothing more than an infomercial, with banners and sidebars all hawking that latest thing. It's a taxonomy of greed, infinitely recycled.

Should we expect anything different from Frank and Keely? Can truth and salvation ever be found?

(the Commentator)

72

Scene 14

DR. MATTHEWS (completes his monologue about Porter Jones):

Four years after Porter got out of federal prison, I got a call from a public defender in Albuquerque, New Mexico. Her name was Alba Woods. She asked me if I knew Porter.

(DR. MATTHEWS acts out the phone call)

DR. MATTHEWS: *Yeah. I know him.*

ALBA WOODS: *He says he was sexually molested by a police officer. Is that true?*

DR. MATTHEWS: *Yes. I have all the paperwork.*

ALBA WOODS: *Would you be willing to tell that to a jury?*

DR. MATTHEWS: *Why a jury?*

ALBA WOODS: *Porter Jones has been arrested for a terrible, terrible crime. He kidnapped and raped a 10-year-old girl. Will you please, PLEASE, tell the jury that he did it because of that cop?!?*

DR. MATTHEWS (Loudly): *I'm not going to do that! It's over. As hard as it may be for you to hear this, it's over. I* can't tell you how many times we bailed Porter out of Juvi. And the misery and heartache of watching him blow through the money – only to end up in prison for armed robbery.

This guy thinks he's immune from punishment. I'm done. He's on his own. No agonized tributes to redemption. This is about accountability. He's on the hook for this one.

DR. MATTHEWS (Looking directly at the audience):

Porter Jones was convicted and given a 100-year sentence without parole.

Witnesses saw him kidnap the little girl off the street. The police immediately gave chase. Up and down a windy mountain road. Porter is driving so fast that he goes off a cliff and rolls down into a ditch. Police don't realize it at first; they keep on driving.

Nobody is hurt. Porter climbs out of the car. It's real quiet. He thinks he's home free. He then rapes the little girl in the upended car.

Can you believe that?

CRYING 4 KAFKA performs the song
"THE SAINT OF FUCKED-UP KARMA"

(Porter Jones)

THE COMMENTATOR:

There's no merit in using any explanation that makes deplorable actions excusable. The whole thing with Porter Jones sickens me.

(Sings a capella)

I've come to where I dread,
The words inside of my head.
Blaring an endless song,
Distant faith so far gone.

Are we supposed to avoid involvement because of the hassles of confrontation? Is downtime the ultimate arbiter of commitment and resolution, as if only when the stars align themselves we do the right thing? Must we also synchronize our watches?

I don't want this to be an unending soliloquy, an acrid stream-of-consciousness that vacillates between pleading and preaching. I'd rather this musical be understood as a fine-grained appreciation of the complications in human lives, Frank's and Keely's in particular, and the necessity of making conscientious choices.

Barriers first feared are best crossed. (Pauses) And if you play with the devil, you're going to get burned.

THE REPRISE

Introductions of band and actors follow the completion of the musical. Crying 4 Kafka then performs a reprise, the song *A Hell of a Love* (a rewrite of Led Zeppelin's *A Whole Lotta Love*.)

THE END

APPENDIX

(Lyrics to songs in the order of appearance)

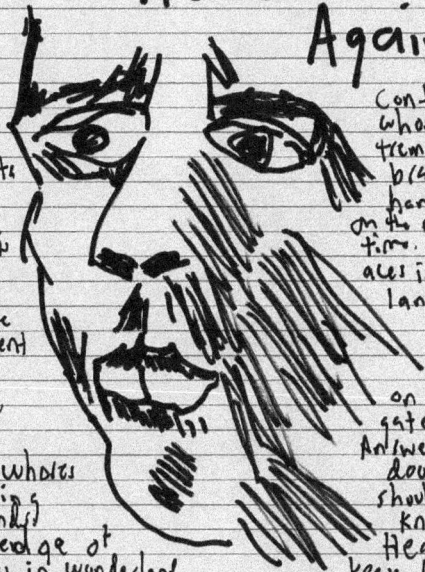

Contemplating Whores Again

Contemplating whores again. I'm too buried in the sand. When forcing smiles today it grows, but it's slippin' out the of my hands one by one knocking on heaven's gates, nobody answering the door. I should've known, hearts silent keep. Love casts shadows on um, long before

Contemplating whores again trembling brackets of hands, standing on the edge of time, casts aces in wonderland. One by one knocking on heaven's gate. Nobody's answering the door. I should've known. Hearts silent keep, Love casts shadows long before.

Contemplating whores again trembling brackets of hands. Standing on the edge of time. Casting aces in wonderland. One by one knocking on heaven's gate. Nobody answering the door. I should've known. Hearts silent keep. Love casts shadows in wonderland

Run Frank Run

I had a dream
the accident

Fucking people make
no sense.

Blackened
world
where rage prevails
desperation

on the rails. Swell of
misery
at night. Deadend streets
and dynamite. Parents sing
A lullaby, voices trembling
bombs fly by.

What the fuck are you doing there,
on your knees without a prayer?
What the fuck are you doing there
on your knees or don't you care? At all.
Do you do you understand. Money money
take my hand. Do you do you understand
money, money ain't like grandad

What the fuck
are you doing
there, on your
knees without a
prayer. What
the fuck are
you doing there on
you knees or don't
you care. At all
Do you do you
understand.
Money money
take my
hand. Do
you do you
understand.
Money
Money
ain't
like
grandad

Run Frank
run
Run Frank
run
Run Frank
run
run Frank
run
run Frank
run
run Frank
run
run Frank
run

run
Frank
run

PM

Holy Roller

Holy Roller with your thunder and awe, tell me more about your fiery well. Holy roller with your venom and hate, punish me now it's never too late. Holy Roller went to save me and then, tie me to the mast and whip me again. Holy Roller with only one thing to say, nothing better then the judgement day.

Holy roller with a book in his hand. I remember the shout of commands. Holy roller in a chorus of cons, singing about Kings and babbling on. Holy roller, keep away from my soul. Demi-gods on stilts with your judgement parole. Holy roller put the barbs in the wire, hidin on pulpits until freedom expires.

There's blood in the rain And it's starting again. Crosses ARE Pointed. And everyone's sinned. They are Burning A place where nobody escapes. It's time for the one who determines his own FATE. x 4

PAN

Dead in the parking
lot at Commuters
liquor store. Fuck,
that's the fate
of all these worn
out morning trou-
badours. Drunk and
alone in a Chrysler
in the freezing
cold. That
hemi headed
engine forever
hidden beneath
the heavy
snow. Wise men in white
at Commuters liquor store.

The hookers wear what's
left of them torn up in
violet and blue. Rattling
them bones and shakin'
fingy at voodoo. Worse
for the wear at 6 in the morn.
Living their ways only life
with the lost and the
forlorn lovelorn work
in an alley or nowhere at all.
At Commuters liquor store

His name was different
everyday, he was a shell of
a man. Shaking like crazy
reaching out to sleep my head.
A dog that can't bark and
a broken pair of shoes.
begging for pennies, a doorway,
or empty bottle of booze

Commuters
Liquor
Store

Nothing to lose at
Commuters Liquor store

"Hey kid, you got a butt."
is all he ever seemed to say. Over,
and over and over until he wheeled
away. Worked as a pharmacist once
upon a time. Now home in garbage
cans looking for that last puff long
time. Mythless meaninglessly to no
one. At Commuters Liquor store

Took me aside and she said, "one
day kid I'm gonna let you climb
inside." Teach me the secrets of the
late-night on a late night highway
ride. Man, she was stunning just
standing there alone. "Frighten"
she said "I'll be your best desired
chaperone." Dancing & singing
for a home at Commuters Liquor
store

Dancing & singing for a home
at
   Commuters
      Liquor
      Store.

Win Big / Lose it All

My old man
He said to me
Frank, you're
gonna, you're
gonna see. You win
Big. **You lose it
all**, you wait and
see.
You know I
laughed. I had
my say. And
with an
old tune I
filed away.
you win big.
You lose it all. You
wait and see.

Give me a rut. I suffered the
foot. Gonna find out what's
coming for you. In a dream
or so it seemed. I'm gonna
find out just what it means.
to climb all the way up
and then, climb all the way
up and then, climb all the way
up and then — turn
back around.

Guitar Solo
My old Man, he
said to me, Frank,
you're gonna, you're
gonna see.
You win
big, **You Lose it all**,
you wait and see X 3

89

Punching At Your Heart

Name/Nom/Nombre _____
Date/Date/Fecha ___ JRN
Assignment/Devoir/Tarea _____

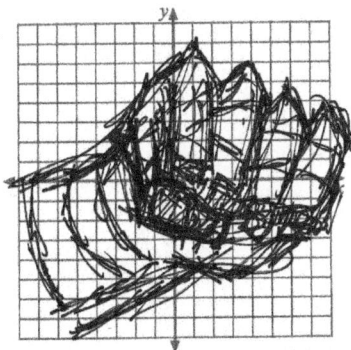

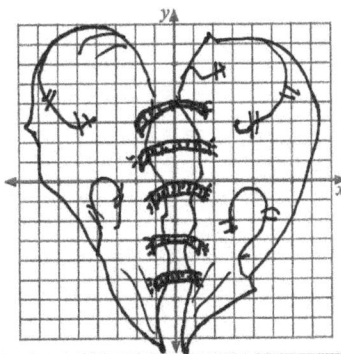

x =
y =

x =
y =

I'm with you - she says it
with a smile.
I'm with you - she changing
her mind
I'm with you - she says it
lyin, down now
Saved up and wasted all the
time

I've always known this
Heart would have no end.
I'm turning back the other
way.
I can't be leanin on your
lips my friend
Now I'm steppin over the
line

Had enough of losing.

Answers are over due
I been watching your hands
I been seein' the truth
So simple illusions
Are they holdin' on to you?
Falling into the dark
PUNCHING AT YOUR HEART

I believe he's selling all his
miracles
I believe he makes his own
rules
I believe he's quoting all
the scriptures
Terrified and living the
fool

Repeat pre-chorus & chorus

91

Hey, I'm NOT SORRY

Name/Nom/Nombre _____
Date/Date/Fecha _____
Assignment/Devoir/Tarea _____

x =
y =

Nights that I'm lonely
cursing wildly in vain
Walk the streets with no
names
Trying to escape the pain

The faces that I love
In the world that I've
known
The lost and all alone
Can never, never go home

Hey I'm not sorry
I don't fit your plan
Hey I'm not sorry
I'm not your kind of man
Hey so sleek, fierce & hot
Hey I'm outside, outside
of the box

x =
y =

Nights that I'm lonely
keep hearing it from you
All that shit I do
And I ain't got a clue

The faces that
I love
So impractical
Damned theatrical
And you're done with it all

Hey I'm not sorry I don't
fit in your plans
Hey I'm not sorry I'm not
your kind of man
Hey so sleek fierce hot
Hey And outside, outside
outside of the box

THE SAINT OF FUCKED UP
Fucked
KARMA

The saint of fucked up
Karma, came to me in a
dream. Angel in a
crosswalk. A legend in
extreme. Fire broke
out within him. While shining
in the sun. I'm going blind
he shouted, walking on the run.
The saint of fucked up Karma
has paralyzed the street again
Round and round and round
he shouts, eternity at 10. We
know that faust was normal
but what about this sage?
free to roam the blvd,
but trapped inside a cage

The saint of fucked up
Karma, came to me in
a dream. Angel in a
crosswalk, a legend in
extreme fire broke out within
him, while shining, in the sun,
I'm going blind he ~~shouted~~
shouted, walking on the run.

The saint of fucked up karma
Dark from within, preaching
~~the truth~~ the truth,
At the crossroads of our sins.
Preaching the truth
At the crossroads of
our SINS PPA

95

OF A HELL LOVE

You've been lying. I'm not crying. I don't give a shit where hearts are flying. Way done inside, bloody hell of a night. You gotta scream when you. You gotta scream when you come. Oh I. WANT A HELL OF A LOVE
x 4

you've been cheatin' and mis-treating. I don't give a shit where hearts are beating. Way down inside. Bloody hell of a night. you gotta scream when you come. you gotta scream when you come. Oh I. WANT A HELL OF A LOVE
x 4
SOLO

you've been cheating And mis-treating. I don't give a shit where hearts are beating. Way done inside. Bloody hell of a night. you gotta scream when you come. You gotta scream when you come. Oh I. WANT

A HELL OF A
LOVE
x 6
Lovvvvvvv vvvv
vvvvvvvvvvv vvv
vvvvv vvvve...

the author
march 1964

www.ingramcontent.com/pod-product-compliance
Lightning Source LLC
Chambersburg PA
CBHW021134020426
42331CB00005B/768